Who Found Who?

By Halina Schafer

An Imprint of Third-Career Press, LLC
Columbia, SC

This is a story about adventure, trust and love.

He always lived alone in a small place and was happy!

Every day he got food, played and learned.

But then...

"Who Found Who?" is an "Easy Reader" for children ages six through nine (1st through 4th grade). It is a story that will keep children engaged whether being read to or reading for themselves.

Sharing a story and asking each other questions sparks their interest and imagination, while challenging their critical thinking skills. Some questions might include:
- Did you ever get lost?
- Who helps you when you are hungry or thirsty?
- How do you think "Georgie" felt at the beginning of the story? And at the end?
- What would you do to get help?

Most parents will want to read the story with the child the first time. Older children will be able to navigate the multi-syllable words, perhaps with some help at first.

Thank you for letting me be a part of this child's early learning experience! It is my hope that they develop a love of reading that leads to success in school and beyond.

Halina Schafer, MSW, LCSW-R (Retired)
Author

Dedication: To all new readers: Ask for help when you need it. Then learn about the word. What does it mean and how do you use it? The more words you learn and understand, the smarter you become. I hope you always want another good story to read!

Remembering Fred who was also brave, even if he was a "scaredy" cat.

Copyright (text and art) © 2018 by Halina Schafer

Artwork is original by Susan E. Harkey, Artist and Art Teacher, purchased for the exclusive use of Halina Schafer, Author.

All rights reserved. No part of this publication may be reproduced, distributed or transmitted in any form or by any means, including photocopying, recording or other electronic or mechanical methods, without prior written permission.

Third-Career Press, LLC
212 Magnolia Bluff Dr.
Columbia, SC 29229
www.third-careerpress.com

Summary: Georgie's adventure goes from fun to fear, after leaving his cage and getting out in the wild. To get help, he must trust Hali.

ISBN 978-0-9988731-1-4 (Softcover - First Ed.)
 [1. Juvenile-easy reader;2. problem-solving; 3. pet adoption;4. birds]

Chapter 1 - An Adventure

Somehow, he got out! Not just out, out in the wild!

This new space was **BIG** and he was just a little guy. It was fun and scary.

"Oh boy, I see everything!"

But, everything looked so different. This was his first time **being** outside and flying.

It was very hot that day. He stopped to rest.

"Oh, look!" He saw food. A lot of food and it tasted good, but after just a few bites...

"Uh-oh!"

"Squawk!"

There was another bird trying to sit and eat. He was **bigger** and **blue** and loud!

What was he saying? He just did not understand.

He stopped for a drink of water, then he flew some more.

Next, he saw a big, red noisy thing below. It was digging up all the dirt.

He wondered if he could find something to eat down there?

He found only a few pieces of hard corn in the dirt. So, he flew some more.

It seemed to be getting dark.

That was scary. Where he lived before, someone covered his cage when it was dark outside. It felt safe and quiet.

"This looks like a place to sit and close my eyes to rest. I'm so tired...

"Zzzzz"

Chapter 2 – All Things New

"Ka – Caw!"

"What is that noise? Oh my, a bird is yelling!" It was time to go. It was getting light out.

He was very hungry and thirsty. He needed to find food and water. So, he flew up high and saw many things below. This time he landed in a field and ate bugs and worms. He did not like them. He flew some more.

He tried to land where there was some water.

A person came out and yelled, very loudly, "Mary, come look what just came in our yard!"

Up he flew again. He thought about how nice it was when people gave him food and water.

After flying for a long time, he was tired again.

First, he landed on a tree branch and looked down. He saw more water and flew toward it.

Just as he landed on the ground, he heard a strange noise close by...

"**Hiss!**" It was a snake! He had never seen one before, not even a corn snake. It looked scary!

As he flapped his wings to go up, he saw a low branch and started to land there. After all, it was off the ground and his wings were so very tired. But...No! No! No! It was the snake with part of its body lifted so it could see him! He flew up even faster!

He was so tired, he knew he needed to rest right now! It was getting dark, again. So, up to a high tree he flew, just as rain started to come down. He moved closer to the tree trunk and held tightly on the limb so the wind and the rain didn't bother him.

All this flying took too much energy.

Even though he was so very, very hungry, he knew it was time to sleep...

Chapter 3 – What Next?

This day was sunny and warm. Off he went to find food.

"I wish I knew where I was or which way to go," he said. He saw a place that looked like another pond.

"I'll go there."

"Hey! There's no water here!"

At least he could rest for a bit.

He thought, "Maybe if I talk to myself, I won't feel so scared. Being alone is no fun now."

Next, he thought, "What should I do? If I could just find a person to help me, I would not be scared!"

Then, he said it out loud:
"Squawk! Chirp-chatter! Squawk!"

First, he heard something. Then, he saw someone! He did not want to be afraid.

"I will behave my best!"

Then, he said, "I think she is talking to me!"

She came closer and kept talking quietly.

"I am too tired to be afraid right now," he said to himself.

She talked to him and he chattered back.

He didn't know what she was saying, but he thought, "She seems nice. I like the way she talks to me."

Then, she said, "Hello there! Aren't you beautiful!"

Uh-oh, she was starting to move away! "What should I do?"

He decided to follow her.

She went up some steps, then stopped. He flew and stopped behind her.

She talked to another person he could not see. He got scared

He flew back to the other spot to wait. He did not want to leave her.

She came back and started to talk, but all he could see was **FOOD!** Very slowly, she brought her hand up with the food.

She talked to that voice and soon the other one was coming outside. So, he flew to the next house to watch...and wait.

Next, she put something down where he had been sitting. She looked up at him and said, "Come," and he did! He knew what that meant: Go to that person!

He saw the water and drank. She gave him more of that "bread" food.

He said, "Thank you," in his own way.

She kept talking softly as the other person came out, then went away again.

He kept liking her more and told her: "Chatter, chirrup, squawk!"

The other person came out where he could see him, but not too close.

She said, "I will be very kind and gentle, as her hand was coming closer. He knew that meant "step up," as he was taught So he did! He was so glad he found her!

Chapter 4 - An Inside Story

She put him in a much smaller house than the one he snuck out of, but it was okay!

The people kept talking to each other and to him. She gave him more food to eat and water to drink.

He thought, "This is great!"

She said, "I will help you."

Somehow, he knew that. But now what?

"Uh-oh, I don't see her! Where did she go? When she came back, she said she, "put up a sign to see if anyone lost you." Then she left again to call a friend who had birds.

"Can I come with you?" he asked in his own way. Then, another person came. He talked nice, too. He showed her something.

She was happy and said, "This is real bird food."

Each time she went away and came back, it made him feel happy.

He thought, "I do like it here! I feel happy and safe.

He thought about the birds, the rain storm and the snake. He thought about how happy he felt now. He squawked and chattered

Later, they all went inside the house. They talked to each other a lot!

But, there, was something that made him nervous ...

Chapter 5 – What Are They?

She calls them "cats". It was strange, because they would walk right by and didn't even seem to notice.

That night, he went to sleep feeling safe and not hungry or thirsty. And soon, he had a much bigger house, called a cage

There were lots of things to play with and look at, in there, and he came out to play with her, too.

She told him, "I'm so happy I found you!"

"This is your new home and family, including the two, fat, lazy old cats."

No one could say where he came from, so Hali and John decided to keep him. Now, his name is "Georgie," and he is learning more each day. If you listen closely, he says "jaw-gee" and "Wazzup?" when Hali or John come into the room. He can say "thank you," even if it does sound like "dee-doo." And, when Hali laughs, Georgie does, too.

Georgie is never out of the cage when a cat is loose. He does keep an eye on the cats, but, mostly, they sleep.

His favorite foods are pasta, snap peas and most fruits.

No one can be sure, though...
"Who found Who?"

What do you think?

Facts about Quaker Parrots (Ask an adult to read this with you.)

Although "Hali" tried, there were no responses from any owners or veterinarians (animal doctors). There is no way to be sure why "Georgie" was outside. Quakers are very smart and can learn to do something by watching. It is possible he opened his own cage, which started this adventure. Hali had no idea how many days Georgie might have been out, alone. The story is true, except for all the things Georgie said. Those came from Hali's imagination.

It was very clear that Georgie had been hand-raised (by watching his reaction to Hali). In some states it is illegal to own a Quaker parrot, as wild flocks are considered a threat to crops. When Hali started to search the internet for information on this type of bird, she learned it was okay to keep him where she lived, along with lots of other information about this breed.

She learned about behaviors, foods to feed and much more.

Rescue Animals:

Taking any animal found outside means you must know how to do this. Hali had a friend / parrot owner confirm her belief that Georgie was not "wild." He liked being handled, being in a cage, and on a schedule.

Hali continues to learn the best ways to keep Georgie healthy and safe, because he can live 20 years or more!

Teaching a parrot is much like teaching a child. You need patience, time and repetition. Quakers are very social animals and want to be around "their family." Like a baby, they will squawk very loudly, if they don't like something. They can bite if they don't want to do something. And, they can get "cranky," especially at bedtime. But, once his cage is covered, Georgie goes quietly to his high perch in the cage, where he sleeps until the next morning.

If you see an animal wandering around near your home, stop and get an adult to help you **before** you decide to touch, feed or adopt a stray animal. Your family must agree, especially if your plan is to take it inside your home.

It is always best to "adopt" a pet from a rescue shelter!

Georgie has been a part of the family for over a year, making this a "Happy Ending!"

If you are a child or parent who enjoyed this story, please let me know at:
www.third-careerpress.com or
Halina Schafer, Author
(on Facebook)
by leaving a review, a post or an email.

We would love to hear from you!

www.ingramcontent.com/pod-product-compliance
Lightning Source LLC
Chambersburg PA
CBHW051555010526
44118CB00022B/2713